ANGELIQUE PARKER

Remedies to a Delightful Marriage

The Delights of Being Married

First edition

This book was professionally typeset on Reedsy.
Find out more at reedsy.com

Contents

1

Introduction

The pages in this book will provide marriage couples with eight remedies to utilize and maintain a delightful marriage. Marriages are dynamic relationships and overtime are confronted with environmental forces which may disrupt the married couple relationship and cause them to cope with unwarranted behavior in their marriage. There are not any predetermined guidelines to follow once you are married; however , employing practical remedies can help salvage your marriage.

Married couples need to maintain happiness in their marriage in order to have a delightful marriage. Every married couple wants a fairytale relationship that resembles infinite happiness and perfection but we all know that no marriage is perfect. In order to preserve the happiness in your marriage both partners have to put in the day-to-day. These remedies that you learn, you have to keep practicing to move onward to safeguard your marriage.

You must tell yourself that divorce is out of the question to fight for your marriage. Center your thoughts around committing to make your relationship stronger and dedicating time and effort to make it work. Avoid thinking about having a life without your partner. Introduce marriage counseling that would offer guidance to align the relationship back in place so that the spouses can work together to experience greater joy in their marriage and exercise these joyful habits that resembles the reason why you decided to unite in marriage.

2

Commitment in Relationships

Commitment is a consensus from both partners who promise to be loyal to each other and willing to provide time and energy to have a prosperous marriage and to grow in love. It is painful when you feel no emotional connection to your spouse. The trust is weakened and erodes the happiness in the marriage. Recognizing the early signs of emotional detachment from your spouse can prevent your marriage from progressively becoming worse. To turn an unhealthy marriage around, do things that would enhance your relationship, do something your partner enjoys i.e., show interest in their hobbies or pick up on the fun things they like to do.

Initiate daily greeting your spouse with a different form of physical touch. A soft kiss on the lips or cheek, a gentle face touch or hand holding can boost your connection with your spouse. The physical closeness can rekindle the passion to help keep the marriage alive. Exchanging memories of passionate moments provide a way to grow closer and an affectionate touch can rejuvenate the spark you once enjoyed with your spouse. To spice up the physical connection, make plans to spend time together to increase the intimacy which allows you to make new memories and increase your happiness.

There are many reasons why married couples grow apart over time. It is an effort from both partners to liven up the relationship and be sure to make progress to bring the relationship back together.

3

Regular Communication

Communication is essential to helping a married relationship remain strong and united. Every marriage has arguments regardless if they are large or small but learning how to communicate effectively can help block unacceptable behaviors that can over time progress into serious issues. Having regular meaningful communication with your spouse will build trust and understanding in turn, elevate the relationship with your spouse. Actively listening to your spouse makes the foundation stronger and stimulates sympathy and closeness.

The communication channel should always stay open. It drives the love in the relationship to a healthy connection in your marriage. Letting each other know how much attention and affection is being displayed will help the relationship overcome the difficult times. Keeping the lines of communication open could shield couples from holding back by expressing their ideas and spending less time together.

It is known that non-verbal communication can aid in communicating in a married relationship. Without saying a word can help express your affection towards your spouse. Using your non-verbal communication assists with displaying how you feel or the mood of your partner. Surprise your spouse with a thoughtful gift i.e., small items, a massage session or leave a sweet note for him/her to read. This ensures that your spouse is not being ignored and is loved. Blended with devotion and unity, you will be able to strengthen your intimate relationship with both verbal and nonverbal communication connections.

4

Share Financial Expenses

One of the major conflicts between married couples stem from financial disputes. Insufficient money is one of the fundamental causes of marriages to suffer and drift towards deterioration or divorce. Your finances should be held to those same high standards in how you are expected to be treated in your marriage. A deep dive discussion about how to approach your debt, household expenses, spending habits and future savings should be handled with that same respect.

There should be a compromise from both sides on how to tackle your finances and the responsibilities split equally between both individuals. Upon the mutual agreement on how the household expenses will be shared, open a combined bank account to pay the joint expenses. The spouse that is better with managing the money affairs should have this responsibility.

It is acceptable for married couples to maintain separate bank accounts for enjoyment and personal spending. After all of the household necessities are paid, give discretionary money to each spouse to spend for fun and leisure. This amount should be budgeted and is best to be disbursed in cash to prevent couples from overspending.

Married couples who are serious about cultivating their future goals about their finances and building savings are better positioned to confront any financial conflicts in the future.

5

Give Spouse Space

Creating space within reason is healthy for a marriage. It is essential because it allows each spouse to take care of their own personal needs apart from their spousal needs. Setting healthy boundaries reduces the likelihood of baseless arguments and a chance to focus on yourself. Engage in an open discussion with your spouse about how and why you need this space.

It is normal for married couples to take time to "recharge" away from each other. Spending limited time apart for self care helps each spouse emotionally and physically to maintain their own independence. Your decision to create space between you and your spouse should be respected by both partners and not taken personally. While prioritizing your "me-time" discussion with your spouse, feel open to ask questions if you need clarity for their intentions.

Knowing that you are two different individuals mutually bound by an union, this opportunity gives both spouses a chance to grow and dedicate time to other personal interests and a time to escape from the daily routine responsibilities. It is your decision if you want to do something together or different with your time. For example, exercising together or having a picnic in the park; the wife gets a chance to hang out with her girlfriends; have a spa day and the husband gets to spend time with his buddies, i.e. visit the bar.

Each spouse should share their experiences with one another and reveal how much they were missed. Be mindful to monitor your personal space to avoid distancing apart from each other.

6

Plan Date Night

Nothing brings a happy married couple closer than having date night. Date night is a pre-arranged time for spouses to enjoy their time together outside their daily routines. Date night can help the couple to refresh the romance in their relationship. During your special night, couples should try something exciting that both couples can do to rekindle the relationship.

Participation in date night requires effort from both spouses if they want to keep the relationship spicy. Carving time out for a regular date night can keep the relationship alive and active. Having date nights can improve the intimacy in the relationship which in turn makes new memories. It also shows your affection for your spouse and reinforces your commitment to each other.

Date night can stimulate creativity and strengthen the bond for the couple who are experiencing a dry spell in their marriage. Dry spells are normal in marriages and it does not always indicate that your marriage is in trouble. Married couples can work through the drought in their marriage to build a stronger and happier relationship. Making your marriage a priority means eradicating negative attitudes and replacing it with a positive outlook.

The bottom line is most marriages are unique and any relationship can hit a dry spell if you do not pay attention to your marriage. Date night is one way to give your relationship a sense of newness, back to being enticing and embracing each other.

7

Ask For Forgiveness

It is inevitable for any married couple to not experience disloyalty in their marriage. We know these transgressions cut to the core of the receiving spouse. Leaving the spouse who experienced betrayal feeling vulnerable and embarrassed. Forgiving someone is not easy and who you truly loved and trusted may take time to heal. Being able to offer and receive honest forgiveness is the beginning of the healing process to a successful marriage. Knowing how to handle betrayals can help you overcome your dreadful situation and salvage your marriage.

Practicing forgiveness is a tool that married couples can utilize to release the hurt and shame. A spouse who holds onto resentment builds bitterness and negative emotions which makes it harder to repair the relationship. An open heart and honest communication with your spouse can help get rid of your resentment towards your spouse's wrongdoing. In addition, working with a marriage therapist to help work through your emotions is a huge step to getting past your spouse's misdeeds and back to feeling connected to one another.

Achieving forgiveness in your marriage is the path to a healthy and happier marriage. Forgiving your partner who hurt you challenges you to put the past behind and experience marital healing and happiness again. Couples who think like a forgiving person are willing to remove the negative emotions and change their behaviors to work toward repairing their marriage.

When we are dealt with betrayal, your feelings get hurt, resentment builds and lowers trust. Addressing your resentment helps the couple identify the reasons for being resentful and restoring the love and respect your marriage deserves. Married couples who find healthy ways to repair their fragile marriage, relinquish the cynical attitude and reintroduce the trust are preparing to move forward to a joyful and healthier life.

8

Stop Being Controlling

Being married to a control freak can rapidly change the dynamics in your marriage from being happy to emotional abuse. These are remedies to save your marriage and ways to deal with your controlling spouse. People who exhibit this behavior do not realize they are controlling until it is brought to their attention. It is essential that you know how to recognize the signs to establish healthy boundaries in marriage.

These are signs of a controlling spouse who may berate his/her spouse i.e., constant criticism, always pushy, prohibits delegation. More distributing if your controlling spouse who is exhibiting controlling signs simultaneously and denies that s/he has a controlling behavior. That being so, seeking a marriage therapist for professional help can be the difference between spending your lives together intentionally or separately aiming towards divorce.

Identify the root cause for your spouse's controlling behavior.

With love, address the underlying anxiety that makes your spouse want to exhibit his/her controlling transgressions. Having a sincere conversation with the controlling spouse to explain your level of respect that you expect from your spouse in order to maintain a peaceful and balanced marital relationship with each other.

Power equality is having an equal balance of power in your marriage. Exercise open communication and soliciting marital counseling, you can reclaim emotional control and fix the unhealthy dynamics in the relationship.

9

Happy Ending

If you feel that your marriage is worth fighting for and want to avoid separation and/or divorce these remedies are key resources to help married couples work through their struggles of feeling disconnected and to maintain a healthy and successful lifelong marriage.

10

Resources

5 Reasons Why Date Night is Important – 25 Suggestions – Couples retreats and Online Couples Therapy. (2021, October 8). Retrieved 20 September 2022, from

https://www.couplestherapyinc.com/5-reasons-date-night-important/Beasley, N. (2022, July 26). *10 Signs Of A Controlling Wife And How To Establish Healthy Boundaries | ReGain.* Retrieved 20 September 2022, from

https://www.regain.us/advice/marriage/10-signs-of-a-controlling-wife-and-how-to-establish-healthy-boundaries/Calkins, W. (2021, August 12). *How to Create Space in Your Relationship.* Eugene Therapy. Retrieved 20 September 2022, from

https://eugenetherapy.com/article/how-to-create-space-in-your-relationship/Hunt, P. (2021, October 29). *6 Ways To Grow Closer To Your Partner.* Better Marriages. Retrieved 20 September 2022, from https://www.bettermarriages.org/communication/6-ways-to-grow-closer-to-your-partner/mindbodygreen. (2022, April 1). *What It Really Means To Have Physical Touch As Your Love Language*. Mindbodygreen. Retrieved 20 September 2022, from

https://www.mindbodygreen.com/articles/physical-touch-love-languageShelly Gigante. (n.d.). *How to share finances in marriage: The mutual payoff*. January 20, 2022.

https://blog.massmutual.com/post/mutual-money-marriageThompson, V. (2022, August 25). *How Do Married Couples Handle the Finances of a Homemaker?* Budgeting Money - the Nest. Retrieved 20 September 2022, from

https://budgeting.thenest.com/married-couples-handle-finances-homemaker-30753.html Ways to Deal with Resentment in a Relationship. (2021). *Lori Lawrenz*.

https://psychcentral.com/health/ways-to-stop-resentment-from-ruining-your-relationship

www.ingramcontent.com/pod-product-compliance
Lightning Source LLC
LaVergne TN
LVHW020547160826
845677LV00015B/4256

* 9 7 9 8 3 5 5 0 4 4 0 1 5 *